SUSHI

Simple and Delicious
SUSHI

Ryuichi Yoshii

APPLE

Contents

Introducing Sushi

The Japanese believe that food should satisfy all the senses. Their food is always prepared with great care, using the freshest ingredients in ways that delight both the eyes and taste buds. The enormous number of sushi restaurants outside Japan attests to the popularity of this appetizing food.

Fish and rice is the staple diet of the Japanese people. Sashimi, which means "raw" in Japanese, is usually served as an entree. (Sashimi generally refers to the delicately arranged plates of raw seafood and sliced fresh fish that are served with soy and other dipping sauces.) Sushi, pronounced "zushi" when it follows a vowel, is the main course or the penultimate dish in a Japanese dinner, served prior to dessert. Sushi is vinegar-flavored rice either topped with sashimi, omelettes or vegetables, or rolled with a variety of fillings inside dark green nori seaweed. Wasabi, a spicy condiment, pickled ginger (gari), and soy sauce are usually served with sushi. Miso soup may also be served with sushi.

To eat sushi, use your chopsticks (or fingers) to pick up the sushi piece and dip the end of the topping into the soy sauce. (Do not dip the rice in the soy sauce as you will taste only soy, not the delicate flavors of the topping and rice.) Put the sushi in your mouth with the topping side down, so that the topping meets your taste buds. Before eating another piece of sushi, eat a slice of pickled ginger to clean your palate, and have a sip of tea. Japanese green tea removes the oiliness of fish. Nowadays, people also drink beer, wine or sake, the traditional Japanese drink made from fermented rice, with sushi.

Sushi is a simple, light and healthy food. Raw fish and seafood contain many vitamins and minerals, a high amount of health-giving omega-3 fatty acids and little cholesterol. There is an enormous variety of sushi in terms of shapes and ingredients. This makes sushi both so complicated that it takes years for the professional chef to master the technique and easy enough to be created at home by you.

RIGHT *Temaki-zushi (see pages 40–41):*
California roll-style (left), Unagi eel and cucumber (right)

Equipment and utensils

The following items are recommended for making sushi and are obtainable from Japanese specialty stores and some larger Asian supermarkets. In many cases, you may obtain suitable substitutes from your kitchen cupboards.

BAMBOO ROLLING MAT (MAKISU) The simple rolling mat used for making sushi rolls. It is made of thin strips of bamboo woven with cotton string. After using, scrub the mat with a brush and dry it thoroughly, otherwise it may become moldy. The best size is 12 x 12 inches (30 x 30 cm), but smaller ones are available.

CHOPSTICKS (SAIBASHI) The chopsticks used for cooking. They are two to three times longer than those used for eating. Cooking chopsticks are extremely useful, once you have mastered the technique. They enable you to manipulate food using only one hand. You will also probably want to have several pairs of chopsticks for individual use when serving sushi and sashimi.

FAN (UCHIWA) An uchiwa is a flat fan made of paper or silk stretched over light bamboo ribs, and is traditionally used for cooling and separating the sushi rice. While it is delightful to own an uchiwa, a piece of heavy paper or cardboard will do the job just as well.

FISH SCALER When cleaning and preparing fish at home, it is easiest to use a scaler, available from a fish market. Simply draw the scaler up the body of the fish, working from tail to head. Do not use the back of a cleaver as a substitute, as you run the risk of bruising the fish.

GRATER Sushi chefs use a length of sharkskin for grating wasabi root; for grating pieces of ginger and daikon, they use a ceramic bowl that has small teeth on the surface. If you are using a straightforward household grater, a flat one made of stainless steel is most suitable. Be sure to choose one that is comfortable to hold and has closely packed, sharp teeth. When using the grater, particularly when grating ginger, use a circular motion.

PLATES FOR SUSHI When serving sushi, you need a set of plates that are as flat as possible. If the rim of a serving plate is curved or ridged, as is common with Western-style crockery, the presentation of the sushi will not be as attractive and they will probably fall over.

RICE-COOLING TUB (HANGIRI) The broad, wooden hangiri, generally made of cypress, is designed specifically for cooling sushi rice. It gives the rice the ideal texture and gloss. A nonmetallic flat-bottomed bowl can be substituted; the bigger the bowl the better, as you will then be able to stir and separate the rice grains properly. To store a hangiri, wash it well, dry it carefully, then wrap it in a cloth and store it face downward in a cool, dry place.

RICE MAKER An electric or gas rice maker is highly recommended for cooking rice, as it will control the temperature and cooking time to give perfect rice every time. Otherwise, you can use a heavy pot with a tight-fitting lid.

SQUARE OMELETTE PAN This square pan, about 1 inch (3 cm) deep, is traditionally used for making sushi omelettes. A thick pan that retains heat is ideal, but can be heavy to handle. You can substitute a conventional round skillet about 10 inches (25 cm) in diameter and trim the sides of the omelette once it has been cooked to make it square.

WOODEN RICE PADDLE (SHAMOJI) This is traditionally used for turning and spreading sushi rice when cooling it, but any kind of broad, flat utensil will do the job. You can use a large wooden spoon or a wooden spatula. Because wood tends to absorb flavors, it is best to use your chosen spoon exclusively for sushi rice. Before using a wooden spoon for sushi rice, wet it thoroughly, or the rice will stick to it.

Sushi ingredients

Japanese people, on the whole, love to live in harmony with nature and therefore favor eating fresh foods in season. In keeping with this attitude, and for the best results, use the freshest foods possible when making sushi.

AJI-PONZU A yellow-colored vinegar that tastes particularly good with salmon. Ponzu is the name of a ready-made lemon and soy dipping sauce.

AKA OROSHI Japanese red chili paste. This is mixed with grated daikon radish and used as a garnish for white-fish sushi. Do not substitute other types of chili paste, as they will probably be too pungent.

BONITO FLAKES (KATSUO BOSHI) These sandy brown flakes of smoked, dried and fermented bonito fish are used to make dashi, a basic Japanese stock. Instant dashi (hon-dashi) are granules of bonito that are added to water to make the stock.

CUCUMBER Japanese cucumbers are about 6–8 inches (15–20 cm) long. They are less watery than American cucumbers and have fewer seeds, firmer insides and softer skins. If you can't find them, use European (hothouse) cucumbers. Buy firm-skinned cucumbers with a medium green color. Cut into 2–4 inch (5–10 cm) lengths before slicing. Cucumber is often used as a filling in sushi rolls and as cut plate decorations.

DAIKON RADISH A Japanese giant white radish with a smooth skin, at least 20 in (50 cm) long. Daikon is less pungent than many radishes. Look for firm, shiny ones with smooth skin and straight leaves. Peel them deep enough to remove both the skin and fibers beneath it. Cut into 2–4 inch (5–10 cm) lengths before slicing.

ENOKI MUSHROOMS These white mushrooms have long, thin stalks and tiny caps. Choose ones that are crisp and white: Yellowish brown ones are old and should be avoided. Cut off the "roots" at the bottom of the stalks.

GARI Ginger slices that have been pickled in salt and sweet vinegar. They are a delicate pink color and are available in bottles and other forms of packaging. The bright red vinegared ginger is not used with sushi.

ICHIMI TOGARASHI A mild Japanese chili powder. Do not substitute with other forms of chili pastes or powders, as they will be too strong. See also aka oroshi.

KAMABOKO Japanese-style fish cakes, available frozen. There are various forms, some of them dyed pink. Kamaboko can be used in chirashi-zushi.

KAMPYO Dried bottle gourd or calabash, used in the form of shavings or ribbon-like strips. Before being used in sushi, kampyo is tenderized and seasoned.

KIMCHEE Korean spicy fermented cabbage. Kimchee is strongly flavored, so use only a small quantity.

KOMBU Dried kelp. This sea vegetable is available in the form of hard, flat, black sheets that have a fine white powder on the surface. Kombu is used to flavor dashi, a basic soup stock, and sushi rice. Wipe the surface of the sheets with a damp cloth before use to remove the powder: do not wash the kombu as you will diminish its flavor. Avoid kombu that is wrinkled and thin.

LOTUS ROOT (RENKON) The crunchy root of the lotus plant is used in a variety of Japanese dishes, including chirashi-zushi. It is peeled, then sliced before cooking. The slices resemble white wheels with holes in them. It discolors as soon as it is cut, so place slices in water to which 1 teaspoon vinegar has been added. It is hard to find fresh lotus root, but vinegared lotus root is available in packets.

MIRIN Sweet alcoholic wine made from rice. Store in a cool, dark place after opening. If mirin is unavailable, use 1 teaspoon sugar in place of 1 tablespoon mirin.

NATTO Fermented soybeans. Natto has a rich flavor, similar to cheese, a pungent odor and a rather glutinous consistency. Many Japanese enjoy natto for breakfast.

NORI Sheets of seaweed used for making rolls. Buy precooked nori, known as yaki-nori, which is dark green. Once the wrapping has been opened, use the nori as soon as possible or store it in an airtight container in a cool place.

SHIITAKE MUSHROOMS These come fresh or dried. The fresh ones should be plump with dark brown caps, cleanly tucked edges and white underneath. They may be parboiled, but taste better if they have been lightly grilled. Use a knife to score an asterisk pattern on the caps, but avoid cutting through the flesh. This allows even cooking and looks decorative.

Soak dried shiitake mushrooms in water for at least 30 minutes before using. The longer they are soaked, the softer they become. Good-quality shiitake mushrooms should become fleshy and plump.

SHISO This aromatic herb, a member of the mint family, is known in the West as perilla. Buy fresh, green leaves. There is also a red variety that is used for coloring and flavoring umeboshi and other Japanese pickles.

SOBORO A pink ingredient made from white fish, used in chirashi-zushi. You can buy it ready-made, in a jar.

SOY SAUCE (SHOYU) This salty sauce is used both as an ingredient and as a table condiment. Dark soy sauce is thicker and often less salty than light soy sauce. Low-sodium products are also available. Japanese soy is best for sushi, as it is naturally fermented and less salty than Chinese soy.

SUSHI VINEGAR (AWASEZU) Sushi vinegar is a mild-tasting vinegar made from rice, specifically for sushi. Other vinegars cannot be substituted, as they are too strong.

UMEBOSHI Salty pickled plums. These are available in bottles and in paste form. Keep opened bottles in the refrigerator.

TOFU A white curd of custardlike texture made from soybean milk. The Japanese "silken" variety has a soft, glossy surface. It is softer and smoother than Chinese tofu. Fresh tofu must be kept in the refrigerator. Once opened, it should be kept in water deep enough to cover it. Change the water at least twice a day; it will keep for 2 days.

WAKAME A type of seaweed available in dried form, reconstituted under running water, used to flavor miso soup.

WASABI Japanese horseradish. Wasabi roots are olive green with a bumpy skin. The best roots are 4–5 years old, 4–6 inches (10–15 cm) long and should be fat and moist. Fresh wasabi is expensive and largely unavailable outside Japan, so powdered or paste formulations are commonly used. The powder is mixed with a small amount of tepid water to make a paste, but prepare only a small quantity at a time as its potency diminishes quickly. You may also find frozen grated wasabi.

Sushi decorations

It is traditional to garnish sushi plates with decorations. These can be elaborate or simple, and many ingredients can be used, including camellia, ivy, shiso, and cucumber leaves; cucumber or carrot decorations; wasabi shapes; and mounds of finely shredded seaweed, daikon radish or carrot. See opposite for some simple ideas, and page 20 for instructions on making a fish rose.

In many restaurants, plastic replicas of bamboo and aspidistra leaf cutouts are used, but you can make your own, using either the real leaves or a substitute. Draw your chosen design onto the leaf and use a small, sharp pointed knife to cut it out. Some traditional designs are shown below.

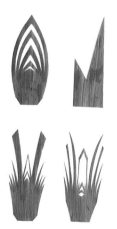
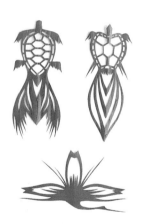

The grasslike cutouts placed in between pieces of sushi, like walls, are named sekisho, after the borders between townships.

A kenzasa cutout resembles a sword (ken means "sword").

Kenshozasa are extremely difficult cutouts to make and need a good deal of practice. Illustrated here are two turtle designs and a crane.

CARROT DECORATION

- Peel and cut carrot into pieces about 1–1½ inches (2.5–4 cm) long. Use the center part of the carrot, not the pointed end.
- Stand the carrot piece on end. Cut a strip of paper ½ inch x 2 inch (12 mm x 5 cm) and fold as shown.
- Place the folded paper on top of a carrot piece and use as a template to cut the carrot into a pentagon shape. Then cut into petals as shown.
- Slice thinly. As an alternative, you can use a metal cutter designed for the purpose.

DAIKON RADISH For each serving, you will need a piece of daikon about 2 inches (5 cm) long. Peel and shred or finely slice, then soak in cold water until ready to use. Drain and squeeze out excess water, then place on plate in a mound shape.

WASABI Wasabi can be placed on the plate in a mound or shaped into a leaf—the vein pattern on top is made with a toothpick. When eating sashimi, do not add wasabi to the soy sauce. Just pick up a small amount of wasabi at the same time as you pick up the fish. This will keep all the flavors separate.

CUCUMBER DECORATION

- Cut a 2 x 1-inch (5 x 2.5-cm) rectangle of cucumber about ¼ inch (6 mm) thick. It should have skin on one side.
- Cut an odd number of slices along the rectangle, each about ⅛ inch (3 mm) wide and 1½ inches (4 cm) long, leaving the final ½ inch (12 mm) uncut.
- Leaving the outermost slices, use your fingers to curl every second slice down into the base of the cucumber.

Preparing Sushi Seafood

The freshest seafood makes the best sushi, for reasons of health, taste and beauty. If you can, purchase from the fish markets, and always buy produce in season. Most fish can be eaten raw, but it is best to choose fish that are commonly used in sushi. Remember, keep all seafood refrigerated until needed.

Selecting Seafood

WHOLE FISH

Whenever possible, buy fish whole and fillet them at home. You can then be sure that the meat is fresh. Use the following guidelines to ensure that whole fish are fresh.

- Check that the eyes are plump, clear and bright. Avoid fish with cloudy pupils.
- The gills should be bright pink-red and look moist. If fish is not fresh, the gills are black-red.
- Overall, the coloring of the fish should be bright or lustrous.
- Stroke the fish to ensure that the flesh is firm and elastic. Stale fish are less elastic and may feel sticky.
- The fish should have a "clean" smell. Avoid ones that have a strong fishy odor.
- Mackerel should have a pointed shape to their stomachs, and the tail on both mackerel and bonito should be upright. A drooping tail shows that a fish is not fresh.

FISH PORTIONS

With bigger fish, it may be inconvenient or uneconomical to buy a whole fish, so buy fillets and smaller cuts. When buying only a portion of a fish, use the following guidelines.

- Fillets should be moist and have a good color.

Fresh, raw tuna

- White fish should look almost transparent.
- Cut tuna flesh should have distinct stripes in it around the belly and be clear red without stripes in other parts.
- The head end of fish is more tender than the tail end.
- With most fish, the back is the most delicious part. Tuna and swordfish are exceptions, in that the tender, fatty belly area is most sought-after.

OTHER SEAFOOD
- When buying shrimp, if they are alive they should be active and of good color. If they are no longer alive, check that the stripes are distinct: they should not be blurred together.
- Touch the tentacles of squid and check that the suckers are still active. The skin around the eyes should be clear blue.
- Sea urchins should be yellow or orange, firm and not slimy.
- Live shellfish are best. When you gently open the shell, it should close by itself.

Filleting fish

- Before cutting the fish, rinse and wipe your cutting board.
- Either keep a bowl of water beside you to wet your knife and then wipe it, or wipe the knife occasionally with a clean, damp cloth.
- There are various methods for cutting different types of fish. The most common of these is the three-part method, or san-mai oroshi style as shown here. This method is used for most fish, apart from larger flatfish and very large fish.
- If you have problems holding the fish, or the bones are scratching you, use a clean kitchen glove on the hand that is holding the fish.
- Try not to handle the body of the fish too much as you may cause bruising. Hold the fish by its head or tail whenever possible.

1. Thoroughly wash the fish and scale it, if scaling is required. Lay the fish down on the board. Use a sharp knife to chop off the head, cutting from under the gills to the top of the head. Cut off the fins on the back and stomach side and hard flaps near the head.

2. With the fish on its side, use your knife to make an incision in the fish belly (only as far as the spine) and slice along the belly side of fish from the head to the anal orifice. With your hands, remove the viscera and, with your knife skimming along the spine, remove the fish stomach. Wash the visceral cavity under running water and then use a brush to scrape off any blood.

3. Put the fish on the board again, and now cut along the back of the fish from the tail to the (missing) head, with your knife tip just running along the edge of the spine.

4. Now let the knife go all the way through, and run it along the length of the fish and lift off the fillet.

6. Any remaining bones in the fillets or around the visceral area should be plucked or trimmed away.

5. Turn the fish over and then slice along the fish back from head to tail, skimming along the spine. Slice along the belly side from tail to head, letting the knife go all the way through to cut the second fillet.

7. You now have three parts: two fillets and one piece consisting of the skeleton and the tail.

Skinning fish fillets

Fish such as mackerel, bonito, sea bream and garfish may be eaten with their skin on. Salmon, tuna, swordfish and cod are usually skinned.

- Lay the fillet on the board, skin-side down.
- Holding the tail end with your left hand, insert the blade of your knife carefully between the skin and flesh at the tail end.
- Using your left hand to add pressure and to hold onto the fish skin at the tail end, slowly pull the skin and flesh, keeping the knife at an angle without moving it and gently let the knife run along the length of the fillet from tail to head, just skimming along the skin.
- As you work, use the side of the knife to push or roll the flesh away as you remove the skin.

For both sashimi and sushi, fish fillets should be deboned, scaled and, where necessary, skinned. The parts of the fish that are not usable for sashimi and sushi may be used in many other ways, such as the spine for making stock.

You will generally need to cut fish fillets into workable-sized blocks before making sashimi and sushi. The length will depend on the fish being used, but the block should be rectangular in shape, measuring about 3 inches (7 cm) across and $1^{1}/_{2}$ inches (4 cm) high. Slices should be $^{1}/_{4}$–$^{1}/_{2}$ inch (0.5–1 cm) thick. Remember that the slices and resulting sushi should be bite-sized.

FISH ROSE You can make a rose using fish! Slice small, thin slices of white fish, such as silvery skinned mackerel or sea bream (whiting) as

shown on page 21. You can also use tuna or salmon to make the rose. Roll one fish slice into a tight roll for center. Roll another piece around it, and continue adding slices one at a time in this way until you have the size you require.

Sushi cuts

When cutting fish for sushi, always cut with the knife pulling the slice toward you. The flesh should be sliced on the bias along the length of the fish or the fillet to give the best results texturally, visually and for taste. One of the basic cutting techniques is the angled cut, known as sorigiri.

Start with a rectangular block of fish about the width of your hand, about 3 inches (7 cm) across and 1½ inches (4 cm) high. With a large fish, such as tuna, you would be able to cut a block like this from the larger block that you had bought. With other fish, such as salmon, try to cut the fish into a block, although the ends and sides may not be particularly even. With salmon or white fish, you can often cut following the existing angle of the fillet.

Measure about 1½ inches (4 cm) in from the top and slice off a triangular piece to make an angled edge to work with. (Any scraps can be used in rolled sushi.) With your knife on a slant to match the angle of the working edge of the block, cut slices about ¼–½ inch (6 mm–1 cm) thick. The remaining piece of the block will also be triangular.

This method is also used with smaller filleted fish, adjusting the knife angle to suit the fillet. With fish such as tuna, the resulting slices will be uniform and rectangular. With smaller fillets, you may have triangular edges or thinner slices. Sometimes you may need to use more than one slice for a piece of nigiri-zushi.

Preparing Sushi Rice

The first step in making sushi is to prepare the rice. It is well worth buying an electric or gas rice maker, as it reduces the process of making rice to the simple press of a button. The following method is for Japanese-style rice, to which a vinegar dressing is added. (See pages 24 and 25 for vinegar preparation.)

Steaming rice

Makes about 8 cups
5 cups (2¼ lb/1.1 kg) short-grain rice
5 cups (40 fl oz/1.25 L) water
1-inch (2.5-cm) square kombu, or reserved kombu
from Number-One Dashi, see page 60 (optional)
½ cup (4 fl oz/125 ml) sake (optional)

Put rice in a bowl that is at least twice the volume of rice and add cold water to near top of bowl. Stir rice briskly with your hands to remove any dirt. Cover rice with your hands as you carefully drain away cloudy water. Repeat process twice more. By third time, water should be clear. (Avoid washing rice too many times, as it removes starch and nourishment and also breaks grains.)

Place rice in a colander to drain. In summer, it will need about 30 minutes, in winter, 1 hour. If using an electric rice maker, place rice and 5 cups (40 fl oz/1.25 L) water in the rice maker and turn on. Machine will cook rice and tell you when it is ready. If using an electric or gas stove, place drained rice and water (plus kombu for additional flavor, if desired) in a heavy-bottomed saucepan and cover with a tight-fitting lid. Bring water to a boil over medium heat. To ensure that rice grains are properly cooked through, do not remove lid throughout entire cooking process. When water boils, increase heat and boil for about 3 minutes. If the pot boils over, adjust heat. Reduce heat to medium and boil for 5 minutes. Reduce heat to low and boil for 5–10 minutes.

Cooking sushi rice in a rice maker

Remove from heat and remove lid (water should no longer be visible). You may wish to follow the practice of some sushi bars and add sake to rice before removing it from heat. This makes rice puff up and adds flavor.

Place cheesecloth or clean kitchen towel over rice, put lid back on and let stand for 10–15 minutes to finish cooking. Remove kombu, if used.

Preparing the vinegar

- While rice is cooking, prepare vinegar dressing, using one of the sets of ingredients on the left.
- Place vinegar and salt in an enamel saucepan and whisk constantly over low heat until salt dissolves.
- Add sugar and whisk constantly to dissolve. Do not let mixture boil.
- Remove pan from heat when the heat is uncomfortable for your hand.
- If made ahead of time, keep dressing in a closed jar in the refrigerator.

Osaka style vinegar dressing

½ cup (4 fl oz/125 ml) sushi vinegar
1 teaspoon rock or sea salt
3 tablespoons superfine (caster) sugar

Tokyo style vinegar dressing

½ cup (4 fl oz/125 ml) sushi vinegar
1 teaspoon rock or sea salt
1 tablespoon superfine (caster) sugar

To combine rice with vinegar dressing: Place hot rice in a wooden rice tub or a large, nonmetallic, flat-bottomed bowl.

Spread rice out evenly around tub using a rice paddle or a wooden spoon. Stir rice to separate grains, slicing paddle across bowl rather than stirring.

Make some space in center of rice and slowly add vinegar dressing in center to distribute flavor evenly. (You may not need to use all of dressing. If you use too much, rice will become mushy.)

Continue lifting and mixing rice with paddle, using a slicing motion. Use a hand-held fan to cool rice. Mix, then fan, then turn rice over and fan again. (Your aim is to make rice slightly sticky, with grains separated and evenly flavored with vinegar dressing.)

| *Add the sushi vinegar to the cooked rice* | *Mix vinegar into rice using wooden rice paddle (shamoji)* | *Fan rice to cool as you stir* |

Continue mixing and fanning until the rice reaches body temperature, then stop. If you let it become colder than this, it will harden. Put rice into a rice holder that has a lid and will keep it warm.

Spread a piece of damp cheesecloth or a damp kitchen towel over top of rice and put lid on. (If you need to turn rice that is cold on top and hot on the bottom, or that has become overly compressed, cover your hand with this cloth and then turn rice with your hand.)

Rice is now ready to be made into sushi. Do not refrigerate rice as it will become hard. Sushi rice will not keep for more than 1 day.

Sushi Rolls

Sushi rolls are a simple, easy-to-eat style of food. They are made by wrapping sushi rice and ingredients in nori seaweed and shaping the rolls with a bamboo rolling mat. With a little practice, sushi rolls are quite easy to make.

Thin sushi rolls (maki-zushi) usually have only one type of filling, as the roll is quite slender. Thick sushi rolls (futomaki-zushi) can be rolled in a variety of ways to make decorative patterns in the rice. Experiment by laying the ingredients in differing patterns on the nori.

For making sushi rolls, a bamboo rolling mat is essential. If you try using a length of cloth or plastic wrap instead, the results are likely to be disappointing.

The best-made sushi rolls have the filling in the center, with rice and nori in concentric circles around the filling. While preparing, keep other ingredients, such as wasabi and sesame seeds, in a small dish near you so you can easily reach them when needed.

Judge carefully the amount of filling to place in the rolls. If the rolls are over-filled, the sheets of nori are likely to break. If you want to add more ingredients, thus making a thicker roll, you will need to lay the nori sheet vertically on the rolling mat, giving you a larger area of nori to wrap around the ingredients.

Sushi rolls are always served with gari (pickled ginger slices) and individual bowls of soy sauce for dipping. The type of garnish to serve will depend on the fillings that have been used and on personal taste. For example, white sesame seeds and shiso go particularly well with cucumber rolls.

Sushi rolls should be eaten as soon as possible after they have been made. Nori soon absorbs moisture and becomes soggy, rather like paper, and the rice inside also expands and may cause the nori to split. Sushi rolls will keep for up to 30 minutes if they are rolled in a paper towel and then in plastic wrap.

RIGHT *Inside-out California rolls (see pages 36–37)*

Tuna rolls

Makes 10 rolls (60 pieces)
5 nori sheets
2 cups (10 oz/315 g) Sushi Rice (see pages 22–25)
Pinch wasabi paste
10 strips tuna, 1/4 x 1/2 x 3 inches (6 mm x 12 mm x 7.5 cm)

Cut each nori sheet in half lengthwise, then cut 3/4 inch (2 cm) from bottom of each sheet. You should have 10 sheets, each measuring about 4 x 6 1/2 inches (10 x 16.5 cm).

Place a nori sheet lengthwise on a bamboo rolling mat, shiny-side down, about 1 inch (2.5 cm) from edge of mat closest to you, with equal space of mat on each side of nori sheet. Wet your hands and take a golf ball–sized handful of sushi rice. Gently squeeze rice into an oblong ball and put on center left of nori sheet. Then use your fingers to squeeze rice into a log along center of nori.

1. Spread rice evenly over nori, working from left to right, leaving a 3/4-inch (2-cm) strip of nori on far side uncovered. Build a low ridge of rice in front of this nori strip. This will keep the filling in place. Take a dab of wasabi on your finger and wipe from left to right across center of rice (if you hold your finger at an angle to start and flatten it out at end, wasabi will spread evenly).

2. Place tuna strips along center of rice, over wasabi.

3. Place fingers flat over tuna strips to hold them in place, then use your thumbs to lift up edge of bamboo rolling mat closest to you.

4. Roll rolling mat away from you, pressing tuna in to keep roll firm. Lift rolling mat over slowly until it covers rice and near side and far sides of rice join at ridge, but you still have a 3/4-inch (2-cm) strip of nori rice-free.

Covering roll (but not rice-free strip of nori), hold rolling mat in position and press all around to make the roll firm. Use your index fingers on top and fingers and thumbs on side to press roll together gently.

5. Lift up top of rolling mat and turn roll over a little more so that strip of nori on far side joins other edge of nori to seal roll. Use your fingers to make sure roll is properly closed.

6. Roll entire roll once more, exerting gentle pressure.

7. Slice roll in half, then cut both rolls twice to give 6 equal-sized pieces. Repeat with remaining nori and rice.

RIGHT Tuna rolls

Cucumber rolls

Makes 10 rolls (60 pieces)
5 sheets nori
2 cups (10 oz/315 g) Sushi Rice
(see pages 22 to 25)
3 cucumbers, cut into 1/4 x 1/2 x 3-inch
(6-mm x 12-mm x 7.5-cm) strips
2 teaspoons white sesame seeds

Prepare rolls in same way as Tuna Rolls (see pages 28–31). Cucumber takes the place of the tuna, and white sesame seeds are added. Sprinkle sesame seeds along center of the rice before putting cucumber in place.

Tuna and cucumber rolls

Makes 10 rolls (60 pieces)
5 sheets nori
2 cups (10 oz/315 g) Sushi Rice
(see pages 22–25)
10 strips tuna, 1/4 x 1/2 x 3 inches
(6 mm x 12 mm x 7.5 cm),
see page 21
1–2 cucumbers, cut into 1/4 x 1/2 x 3-inch
(6-mm x 12-mm x 7.5-cm) strips

Prepare rolls in same way as Tuna Rolls (see pages 28–31).

Natto rolls

Makes 4 rolls (24 pieces)
2 sheets nori
1 cup (5 oz/155 g) Sushi Rice (see
pages 22–25)
6 tablespoons natto (fermented
soybeans)
5 shiso leaves, finely chopped
Pinch bonito flakes

Prepare rolls in same way as Tuna Rolls (see pages 28–31).

Tuna and cucumber rolls

Natto rolls

Umeboshi plum rolls

Makes 4 rolls (24 pieces)
2 sheets nori
1 cup (5 oz/155 g) Sushi Rice (see
pages 22–25)
20 umeboshi plums, pitted and
chopped, or 6 tablespoons
umeboshi paste
5 shiso leaves, finely chopped

Prepare rolls in same way as Tuna Rolls (see pages 28–31). If you use umeboshi paste, apply it in the way described for wasabi paste.

Salmon rolls

Makes 10 rolls (60 pieces)
5 sheets nori
2 cups (10 oz/315 g) Sushi Rice) (see
pages 22–25)
10 strips salmon, 1/4 x 1/2 x 3 inches
(6 mm x 12 mm x 7.5 cm)

Prepare rolls in same way as Tuna Rolls (see pages 28–31). If you wish, you can mince the salmon instead of cutting it into strips.

California rolls

Makes 4 rolls (32 pieces)
4 nori sheets
3 cups (15 oz/470 g) Sushi Rice (see pages 22–25)
8 teaspoons ocean trout or flying fish roe
1–2 cucumbers, cut into thin, lengthwise slices
8 jumbo shrimp (king prawns), cooked and shelled (see pages 46 and 47),
veins and tails removed, cut in half lengthwise
1–2 avocados, peeled, pitted and sliced
4–8 lettuce leaves, torn or sliced (optional)

California rolls, as their name suggests, were invented in California, although thick sushi rolls like these ones originated in the Osaka area of Japan.

Lay a nori sheet on a rolling mat and top with sushi rice as for Tuna Rolls (see pages 28–31). Spoon 2 teaspoons roe along center of rice, using back of spoon to spread. Add lettuce if desired. Lay 2 shrimp along center with one-quarter of cucumber strips. Lay one-quarter of avocado slices along center. Add one-quarter of lettuce. Roll nori sheet over ingredients as for Tuna Rolls (see pages 28–31).

Inside-out California rolls

4 nori sheets
3 cups (15 oz/470 g) Sushi Rice (see pages 22 to 25)
8 teaspoons ocean trout or flying fish roe
1–2 cucumbers, cut into thin, lengthwise slices
1–2 avocados, peeled, pitted and sliced
8 jumbo shrimp (king prawns), cooked and shelled (see pages 46 and 47),
veins and tails removed, and cut in half lengthwise
4–8 lettuce leaves, torn or sliced (optional)

Makes 4 rolls (32 pieces)

1. Cover a rolling mat with a sheet of plastic wrap, folding it over edges and attaching it to back of mat. Turn mat over so plastic-covered side is facing down. Lay 1 nori sheet on rolling mat. Use about ¾ cup (4 oz/125 g) rice to cover nori sheet, starting with a ball of rice at bottom and then spreading it out. Cover nori with rice right up to edges. Spread about 2 heaped teaspoons roe over rice, using back of a teaspoon.

2. Pick up rice-covered nori by corners, quickly turn it over and place upside down on bamboo rolling mat.

3. Add lettuce, if desired. Place sliced cucumber along center of nori. Add avocado, then shrimp.

4. With your hands held over base of mat and pressing in on ingredients with your fingers as you go, roll mat over ingredients, leaving 3/4 inch (2 cm) of nori visible at far end of nori end of roll.

5. Press gently to mold roll together. Lift up mat, roll back a little, then roll forward to join nori edges. Use gentle pressure to firm and mold completed roll into shape, either round, oval or square.

6. Using a sharp knife, cut each roll in half, then cut two halves in half again. Then cut four quarters in half to make 8 equal-sized pieces. Cut gently to maintain shape.

Futomaki with kampyo, omelette, soboro and cucumber rolls

Makes 4 rolls (32 pieces)
4 nori sheets
3 cups (15 oz/470 g) Sushi Rice (see pages 22 to 25)
2 oz (60 g) Seasoned Kampyo (see page 61)
1–2 cucumbers, cut into thin slices lengthwise
Shredded, thin omelette, using 3 eggs (see page 57)
Seasoned Shiitake Mushrooms (see page 61)
Shredded watercress, parsley or spinach leaves; bamboo shoots; soboro (optional)

To make, follow steps for making Tuna Rolls (see pages 28–31).

RIGHT *Kampyo, omelette, soboro and cucumber rolls*

DESIGNING FUTOMAKI Just as you can experiment with different fillings in sushi, you can also use fillings to create strikingly decorative sushi rolls. The way you lay out the ingredients on the flat nori sheets and rice will affect the final design of your roll. You may like to use food coloring to dye the rice. In this picture, the colorful rice was wrapped in seaweed first, then rolled again to make one large roll around an omelette. The square shape was achieved by pressing in the bamboo mat to make a square rather than a flat roll.

Sushi Shapes

Sushi comes in a vast array of shapes. The easiest type to make at home is Temaki-zushi, or sushi hand rolls. These cones of nori filled with sushi rice and a variety of other ingredients make excellent party food. On the following pages you will also find other interesting sushi shapes, such as traditional nigiri-zushi.

Temaki-zushi

5 cups (25 oz/780 g) Sushi Rice (see pages 22–25)
20 nori sheets, halved
Wasabi paste

Prawn tempura and lettuce temaki-zushi (left), and tuna and shiso temaki-zushi (right)

Choice of fillings:
Salmon or tuna, minced or cut into 3/8 x 3/8 x 3-inch (1 x 1 x 7.5-cm) sticks
Jumbo shrimp (king prawns), cooked, and shelled (see pages 46 and 47), veins and tails removed, and cut in half lengthwise
Sea urchin or salmon roe
Cooked or smoked fish, cut into 3/8 x 3/8 x 3-inch (1 x 1 x 7.5-cm) sticks
Omelette, cut into 3-inch-long (7.5-cm) strips
Cucumbers, cut into 3-inch (7.5-cm) lengths, then finely sliced lengthwise
Avocado slices
Sliced or torn lettuce leaves
Blanched vegetables such as asparagus, snow peas (mange-touts), sliced onion and carrot
White sesame seeds
Scallions (shallots/spring onions) or chives, finely sliced

1. Pick up a sheet of nori and hold it flat in your left hand, rough-side up. Take a spoonful of rice and place an oblong ball of rice on left side of nori. Flatten out rice and make a groove for other ingredients. With a small spoon, wipe a little wasabi along rice.

2. Add filling or fillings of choice. Here we are adding long slices of cucumber and eel.

3. Fold near corner of nori sheet over filling to make a pointed end.

4. Use fingers to roll nori into a cone shape. Grasp nori to seal roll.

Nigiri-zushi

In Japanese, nigiri means "squeeze." Nigiri-zushi are made by gently squeezing together bite-sized pieces of fish (or other foods) and small balls of sushi rice.

Tips for nigiri-zushi

At sushi bars, you may notice that sushi vary somewhat in terms of quantities of rice, wasabi and other ingredients, as well as the shapes of the rice and the toppings. As your guide to size, remember that sushi is best eaten in a single mouthful, so for each piece use a ball of rice the size of a golf ball and enough topping to cover it. Use a moderate amount of wasabi for richer, more oily fish such as tuna and salmon, and less for mild-tasting seafood such as shrimp, squid and octopus. The important thing for the home cook is to make sushi that stand up and stick together well. We recommend the traditional method for making nigiri-zushi, tategaeshi style—the method is on the following pages. It gives professional results and, with a little practice, is easy to master.

When making sushi, hold your hands comfortably at the level of the top of your stomach, with your elbows just a little in front of your body. Make sure your ingredients are ready and nearby. Cut slices of fish, such as tuna, salmon, sea bream, yellowtail, mackerel and snapper, just prior to making the sushi, using the method on page 21). Have a damp cloth alongside for wiping knives, and a bowl of tezu (water mixed with vinegar), for keeping your hands moist so the rice does not stick to you. (The proportions are 1 cup water (8 fl oz/250 ml) to 1 cup (8 fl oz/250 ml) sushi vinegar.) To wet your hands to the right extent, use your right index finger (if you are right-handed) to wipe tezu on left-hand palm in a circular motion, then clap your right fist over your left hand and wipe the water off your fingers so your hands are just moist. Also have beside you a small bowl of wasabi.

Once you have mastered the tategaeshi method, and tried the various examples provided, you can use your skills to create your own sushi.

RIGHT Thin-omelette (right) and Squid (left) nigiri-zushi with Salmon rose decoration (back)

Nigiri-zushi — Tategaeshi style

With moist hands, pick up a golf ball-sized ball of rice. Gently squeeze the rice to form a rectangular block with rounded edges and sides.

1. Lay fish piece flat in your left hand, across middle joints of your fingers. Use your right-hand index finger to spread a dab of wasabi along length of fish.

2. Pick up the rice you shaped and put on top of fish in your left hand. Gently use your left thumb to press down on top of rice in middle, making a slight depression in rice.

3. Still holding your thumb to rice, turn your left hand over slowly and carefully from the elbow. With your right hand under your left, use your right-hand thumb and index finger to hold piece (along sides of rice).

4. Quickly turn your left hand over so it is under your right hand with palm facing upwards. Place sushi back into your left hand (across middle joints of fingers). With your right hand side-ways (not above fish piece), use your right-hand index finger and thumb to hold and press sides of rice gently.

5–6. To form sushi, you will now use three actions together. These steps should be done in one quick, gentle pressing action, which is then gently released.

• Keeping your left hand relaxed and fingers slightly tilted down, wrap your fingers upwards to hold and press sushi (which will then sit straight if you have tilted your hand down).

• With your left-hand thumb, hold and press end of rice.

• Hold your right-hand index and middle fingers straight and together and use them to gently press down along top of fish.

7. Hold your right hand over top of sushi piece and use your index and middle fingers on far side and your thumb on near side to pick up and turn sushi piece around in your left hand.

8. Repeat previous step, where you quickly pressed sushi with left thumb, left fingers and right-hand index and middle fingers.

9. You should now have a well-formed piece of sushi. If not, turn the piece around once more and press again. With right-hand index finger, quickly wipe along top of fish to make fish shiny.

Preparing jumbo shrimp for nigiri-zushi

jumbo shrimp (king prawns)
sushi rice

1. Wash shrimp under running water and cut off heads. Insert a bamboo skewer or long toothpick along shrimp from head to tail, running along legs of shrimp without touching flesh.

Drop shrimp into a pot of salted, boiling water (use enough salt to make it taste like seawater.) Boiling

shrimp in salted water keeps protein in shrimp. They will sink to bottom and after 3 to 5 minutes will change color and rise to top. (Do not use a lid, or a strong smell of shrimp will remain.) To check that they are cooked, remove one shrimp from water and squeeze gently. If inside is firm, it is cooked.

Quickly place shrimp in ice water. This gives them a good color and stops flesh from shrinking and becoming hard. When shrimp are cold, remove from ice water and place in a colander. To remove skewer, use a screwing motion to avoid breaking flesh. Remove shell from around body, but not tail.

2. To make butterfly cut, lay shrimp down with tail away from you, then cut from head to tail along belly with knife only going halfway in.

3. Use the knife or your fingers to open out and flatten shrimp carefully, without breaking the flesh. Remove vein and rinse shrimp with mildly salted water. Lay on paper towels to drain.

Jumbo shrimp nigiri-zushi

Omelette sushi (see page 57) with nori belt

NORI BELTS If you are using a topping that is prone to slide off the rice, such as omelette, scallops, squid, tofu or snow peas (mange-touts), you may need to use an obi-jime, or a nori belt, to tie the topping on. After forming the nigiri-zushi, take a small strip of nori about ½ x 3 inches (12 mm x 7.5 cm) and use this as a belt to strap the topping firmly to the rice, as shown in the picture. This is called obi-jime-zushi.

Gunkan maki-zushi

Makes 8 sushi
1 nori sheet
1 cup (5 oz/155 g) Sushi Rice (see pages 22 to 25)
Wasabi paste
4 oz (125 g) sea urchin, salmon, ocean trout or flying fish roe

Some ingredients will not stay on top of rice, even with a nori belt. With semi-liquid ingredients, such as sea urchin and salmon roe, it is necessary to wrap the whole sushi within nori sheets to hold it together, gunkan-maki style, otherwise known as battleship sushi. When making gunkan-maki, remember that moist hands are good for touching the sushi rice, but it is best to have dry hands when handling nori.

Because nori is like paper, if you are making various kinds of sushi, leave the making of gunkan maki-sushi until last, otherwise the nori will become wet and may break.

Cut the nori into strips about 1 inch (2.5 cm) wide and 6 inches (15 cm) long. Take a golf ball–sized ball of rice in your hand and gently squeeze it into a rectangular block with rounded edges. Place on a clean board. Repeat with remaining rice.

With one moist hand holding one rice ball, use dry fingers of your other hand to pick up nori sheet. With rough side of nori facing rice, press end of nori to rice (it will stick) and then wrap nori all around rice. Gently press overlapping edge of nori to form a complete ring (or use a crushed grain of sticky rice to hold the ends together).

Dab a little wasabi on top of rice, then place roe on top of rice inside center of ring of nori.

Inari-zushi

Inari-zushi is named after the Japanese god of grains. According to myth, foxes are the messengers of Inari and guard the Inari shrines. Perhaps these sushi are so named because their pointed shape resembles the ears of a fox, or perhaps it is because foxes like deep-fried tofu.

Preparing tofu pouches

Special deep-fried tofu bags, called abura-age-dofu, are sliced open to create pouches for inari-zushi. You will be able to obtain them already cooked from an Asian supermarket. Before you use them, rinse them in boiling water to remove as much oil as possible. The tofu pieces are either square or oblong, and they can be sliced in a number of ways. Square slices can be cut diagonally to make triangular inari-zushi. Oblong slices can be opened out by being cut down the two shorter sides and one long side, then rolled around a filling and tied with strings of cooked kampyo. If you open out a rectangular pouch and then fold the mouth inwards to about half the depth of the pouch, you can make inari that resemble little boats. If you find it difficult to open them, roll the sheets with a rolling pin or slap them between your hands.

As with most other types of sushi, the filling can be varied to suit your personal taste or to accommodate what is seasonally available. Some people add only sushi rice; others like to flavor the rice with roasted sesame seeds, lemon zest, vinegared lotus root or hemp seed. Filling ingredients will need to be finely chopped to fit comfortably within the tofu bag. You may like to try these fillings:
- Sushi rice with carrot, lotus root and cooked shiitake mushrooms
- Sushi rice with poppy seeds and cucumber

Makes 10 sushi

**5 pieces 2 x 4-inch (5 x 10-cm)
or 10 pieces 2 x 2-inch (5 x 5-cm)
thin deep-fried tofu**

**1 cup (8 fl oz/250 ml) Number-One
Dashi (see page 60)**

2 tablespoons superfine (caster) sugar

2 teaspoons sake

2 tablespoons dark soy sauce

**1½ cups (8 oz/250 g) Sushi Rice (see
pages 22 to 25)**

Place tofu squares in a saucepan of boiling water. Boil for 3 minutes to remove excess oil. Remove from water and drain. Put tofu in a saucepan with dashi (use a drop-lid if you have one, a round wooden lid that sits inside pot on top of mixture and allows steam to escape around edges) and bring to a boil over high heat. Reduce heat to low and simmer for 5 minutes. Add sugar and sake, and simmer for 5 minutes. Add soy sauce and simmer for 5 minutes. Remove from heat, lift out tofu and drain.

1. Cut each piece of rectangular tofu in half to make 2 squares; cut square tofu diagonally to make 2 triangles.

2. Open center of each cut triangle or square to make a pouch.

3. With moist hands, take a ball of sushi rice the size of a golf ball and gently squeeze it together. Fill tofu pouch loosely with sushi rice.

4. Wrap edges of pouch around rice to form inari-zushi.

Vegetable Sushi

Japanese people always favor using foods that are in season for their cooking, and the variety of vegetables available through the year provides great scope for the imaginative sushi maker. Vegetables combine well with the delicate flavor of sushi rice, as do various other foods, such as omelettes, tofu and cream cheese.

If you are making a mixed platter of sushi, it is a good idea to make a few vegetable sushi to add color and nutritional value. You can experiment with cooked, blanched and raw vegetables and various garnishes, such as fresh ginger, finely chopped shallots, miso paste and chili seasonings. You can also "Westernize" your sushi with your own variations.

Vegetable sushi often need to be wrapped with a nori belt to prevent the vegetables from falling off the sushi rice.

Avocado sushi

Makes 10 sushi
1–2 avocados, peeled, pitted and sliced
10 nori belts (see page 47)
1 cup (5 oz/155 g) Sushi Rice
White or red miso paste, for garnish

Use 2 slices of avocado for each sushi piece. Make sushi using nigiri-zushi method (see pages 42–45). Wrap nori belts around sushi. Top each with a dab of miso paste.

LEFT Avocado sushi with miso (left), Tofu sushi with freshly grated ginger and shallots (right)

Some of the vegetables used in sushi include asparagus,
snow peas (mange-touts), avocado, eggplant and ginger

Tofu sushi

Makes 10 sushi

8 oz (125 g) firm tofu, drained
1 cup (5 oz/155 g) Sushi Rice
10 nori belts (see page 47)
Grated fresh ginger, minced
    scallions (shallots/spring onions)
    white or red miso paste, or
    mayonnaise, for garnish

Cut tofu into 1/4- x 2- x 21/2-inch (6mm x 5-cm x 6-cm) pieces. Make sushi using nigiri-zushi method (see pages 42–45). Wrap nori belts around sushi. Add garnish of your choice.

Shiitake mushroom sushi

Makes 10 sushi
10 fresh shiitake mushrooms, stemmed
1 cup (5 oz/155 g) Sushi Rice (see pages 22–25)
Rock or sea salt for sprinkling
2 lemons, cut into wedges

Using a sharp knife, score mushroom caps with an asterisk pattern, but avoid cutting through flesh. Grill or broil mushrooms for 1–3 minutes, or until tender and darkened. Sprinkle a little salt on mushroom caps. Makes sushi using nigiri-zushi method (see pages 42–45), placing mushrooms either upside down or right-side up. Serve with lemon wedges. Squeeze on lemon juice before eating.

Eggplant sushi

Makes 10 sushi
1–2 Japanese eggplants (aubergines), peeled
Vegetable oil for deep frying
1 cup (5 oz/155 g) Sushi Rice (see pages 22–25)
White sesame seeds for garnish
1/2 cup (4 fl oz/125 ml) soy sauce
2 tablespoons sugar
1 cup (8 fl oz/250 ml) mirin

Cut eggplant slices into slices measuring 1/4 x 1 1/2 x 2 1/2 inches (6 mm x 4 cm x 6 cm). Brush with oil. Deep-fry eggplant for about 2 minutes, or until soft. Drain and cool. Make sushi using nigiri-zushi method (see pages 42–45). Combine soy sauce, sugar and mirin in a saucepan. Boil to reduce to 1 cup (8 fl oz/250 ml) or 1/2 cup (4 fl oz/125 ml), depending on your taste. Garnish sushi with white sesame seeds and pour a little sweet soy sauce on top.

RIGHT *Shiitake mushroom sushi (left) and Eggplant sushi (right)*

Snow pea sushi

Makes 10 sushi
10 nori belts (see page 47)
1 cup (5 oz/155 g) Sushi Rice (see pages 22 to 25)
20 snow peas (mange-touts), blanched and cooled
Umeboshi paste or mayonnaise for garnish

Make sushi using nigiri-zushi method (see pages 42–45). Wrap nori belts around sushi. Garnish each with a dab of umeboshi paste or mayonnaise.

LEFT Asparagus sushi with mayonnaise and chili powder (left) and Snow pea sushi with miso (right)

Asparagus sushi

Makes 10 sushi
10 asparagus spears, trimmed, blanched and dipped in iced water
10 nori belts (see page 47)
1 cup (5 oz/155 g) Sushi Rice (see pages 22–25)
Mayonnaise and red chili seasoning (ichimi togarashi) for garnish

Cut asparagus into 2–3-inch (5–7.5-cm) pieces. Cut lengthwise if they are thick. Make sushi using nigiri-zushi method (see pages 42–45). Wrap nori belts around sushi. Garnish with a dab of mayonnaise and a pinch of red chili seasoning.

Omelette sushi

Makes 10 sushi
8 eggs, beaten until blended
1/3 cup (3 fl oz/80 ml) Number-one
  Dashi (see page 60)
1/3 cup (3 oz/90 g) sugar
1 teaspoon mirin
Pinch salt
2 tablespoons light soy sauce
vegetable oil for cooking
1 1/2 cups (8 oz/250 g) Sushi Rice (see
  pages 22–25)
10 nori belts (see page 47)

In a bowl, combine eggs, dashi, sugar, mirin, salt and soy sauce. Heat 1–2 tablespoons oil in a square omelette pan over medium heat. Pour excess oil into a bowl nearby, ready to re-oil pan when needed. Pour a thin layer of omelette mixture in pan. Use chopsticks or a spatula to press out any air bubbles. When omelette is firm, loosen it from the sides and fold one-third of omelette from far side toward center. Then fold the double layer over remaining one-third to the side closest to you. Add more mixture, lifting cooked omelette up to let it flow underneath. When firm, fold over as before. Continue adding mixture, cooking until firm and folding, until all the mixture is used.

Remove from heat and use a wooden board that fits inside the pan to press down on the omelette. Turn omelette onto a board and cool. Cut layers into strips and use a nori belt to strap omelette pieces to sushi, nigiri-zushi style. Or, cut into fine shreds and use for sushi rolls as pictured here.

*LEFT Thick sushi roll
(futomaki-zushi) wrapped in
nori and thin omelette sheets*

Sushi in a Bowl

Sushi in a bowl, or chirashi-zushi as it is known in Japanese, is a great one-dish meal that is easy to prepare at home. Chirashi means "scattered", and this is what you do: Fill a bowl with sushi rice and then scatter the ingredients decoratively over the rice. Almost any fish or vegetable can be used—it is up to the cook's imagination as to what it contains. Suggested ingredients for chirashi-zushi include:

- seasoned kampyo (see page 61)
- seasoned shiitake mushrooms (see page 61)
- toasted sesame seeds
- deep-fried tofu (sliced and rinsed in boiling water to remove excess oil, then boiled in $1/2$ cup (4 fl oz/125 ml) Number-one Dashi (see page 60) and $1/2$ cup (4 fl oz/125ml) water until soft)
- tofu cakes
- cucumber
- avocado
- cooked baby shrimp (prawns)

If you wish, you can season the sushi rice used for chirashi-zushi with chopped vegetables, green peas, chopped fresh ginger, gari (pickled ginger slices), soboro, crumbled nori, toasted sesame seeds, tofu or strips of deep-fried tofu, or various sauces. The dish is then called bara-zushi.

1. In a large bowl, spread sushi rice to make a flat bed, keeping rice loosely packed. Add a layer of seasoned kampyo and ginger, covering rice.

2. Add a layer of seasoned shiitake mushrooms and soboro to cover ingredients already in the bowl.

3. Add a layer of shredded nori seaweed and shredded thin omelette to cover the ingredients already in the bowl.

4. Make a decorative display on top with jumbo shrimp and snow peas (mange-touts). Finish off by adding carrot and cucumber decorations.

Make Your Own...

Dashi is a basic ingredient in many Japanese soups, sauces and traditional dishes and can be used as a substitute for Western-style stocks and consommés. It has a delicate, mild fishy flavor. We recommend making your own dashi because of the quality of the final stock, but instant dashi (hon dashi) may be substituted.

Number-one dashi

Makes 4½ cups (36 fl oz/1.1 L)
4½ cups (36 fl oz/1.1 L) water
one 4-inch (10-cm) square kombu
½ oz (15 g) bonito flakes

Use a clean, damp cloth to wipe off white film on surface of kombu. In a saucepan, combine water and kombu. Let soak for up to 2 hours, then place over high heat and bring to a simmer. When stock begins to bubble slightly, after about 5 minutes, check center of kombu. If it is soft, remove kombu from saucepan and set aside. If hard, cook for few more minutes, then remove.

Let mixture come to boil, then stir. Skim off any bubbles or scum on surface. Remove from heat and add a small amount of cold water to lower temperature before adding bonito flakes. (Boiling water makes them smell.) Add bonito flakes to saucepan. Do not stir. Use chopsticks to press the flakes down gently to bottom of saucepan. Let rest for 3 minutes.

Lay a cheesecloth or a clean napkin over a colander and strain mixture into a large bowl to remove bonito flakes. Remove the drained bonito flakes and reserve. If, after tasting the finished dashi, you wish to strengthen its flavor, return mixture to saucepan and simmer for another 5 minutes.

Use leftover ingredients from Number-one Dashi to make Number-two Dashi, a milder, diluted stock.

You can also make a strong miso soup with Number-one Dashi.

Number-two dashi

Makes 4¹/₂ cups (36 fl oz/1.1 L)
**Reserved bonito flakes and kombu
from Number-one Dashi**
4¹/₂ cups (36 fl oz/1.1 L) cold water

Put all ingredients in a saucepan.

Bring to a boil over high heat and cook
for 15 minutes. Remove from heat.
Lay cheesecloth or a clean napkin
over a colander and strain mixture
into a large bowl. Remove drained
bonito flakes. Dashi should be clear.

Seasoned kampyo

³/₄ oz (20 g) kampyo strips
**2 cups (16 fl oz/500 ml) Number-two
Dashi (see above)**
¹/₄ cup (2 fl oz/60 ml) dark soy sauce
1 teaspoon superfine (caster) sugar

To prepare seasoned kampyo, soak
kampyo in water for at least 2 hours,
or if possible overnight. The longer

the soaking, the better the texture.
Place kampyo and soaking water in a
saucepan and boil until translucent
and tender, about 10 minutes. Drain.
In a saucepan, mix together 1 cup
(8 fl oz/250 ml) of dashi, soy sauce
and sugar. Add kampyo to mixture
and boil for 5 minutes. Drain
and set aside to cool.

Seasoned shiitake mushroom

4 dried shiitake mushrooms, stemmed
**¹/₂ cup (4 fl oz/125 ml) Number-two
Dashi (see above)**
3 tablespoons light soy sauce
1 tablespoon superfine (caster) sugar
1 tablespoon mirin

To prepare seasoned shiitake
mushrooms, soak caps in lukewarm

water for at least 2 hours or overnight.
Drain, reserving liquid. Cut mushrooms into ¹/₄-inch (6-mm) strips. In
a saucepan, mix together remaining 2
cups (16 fl oz/500 ml) dashi, light
soy sauce, sugar and mirin. Bring
mixture to a boil, add mushrooms and
simmer for 10 minutes. Remove from
heat and drain mushrooms.

Index

A LANSDOWNE BOOK

Published by Apple Press
Sheridan House
4th Floor
112-116 Western Road
Hove
East Sussex BN3 1DD UK

www.apple-press.com

Copyright © 2002 text, photography and design: Lansdowne Publishing Pty Ltd

Created and produced by Lansdowne Publishing
Text: Ryuichi Yoshii
Photographer: Louise Lister
Designer: Avril Makula
Editor: Joanne Holliman
Production Manager: Sally Stokes
Project Coordinator: Kate Merrifield

ISBN 1 84543 005 0

Set in Trade Gothic, Journal Text, Gill Sans and Neuropol on QuarkXPress
Printed in Singapore by Kyodo Printing Pte Ltd

Cover picture: Tuna, squid and salmon nigiri-zushi
Pictured on page 2: Nigiri-zushi: (Front) Garfish, Shrimp, Swordfish, Unagi eel with
belt, (Back) Salmon, Squid with black sesame, Tuna, Sea bream (whiting), Bonito
Pictured on page 5: Omelette sushi with nori belt